FAMILY TREE SECRETS
&
GENEALOGY SEARCH TIPS

by
Richard Sullivan

1

Other Books
by Richard Sullivan:

The First Ward
The First Ward II: Fingy Conners & The New Century
Driving & Discovering Hawaii: Oahu
Driving & Discovering Hawaii: Maui and Molokai
Reclaim Your Youth

Family Tree Secrets & Genealogy Search Tips
by
Richard Sullivan
Copyright © 2014 by Richard Sullivan

ISBN-13: 978-1501000508

ISBN-10: 1501000500

Montgomery
Ewing

Montgomery Ewing Publishers LLC
HC2 Box 9628
Keaau Hawaii 96749

Hawaii: 808-966-6717
Los Angeles: 323-395-7499

Dedicated to my sister,
Barbara Sullivan

Table of Contents

Introduction

My sister Barbara Sullivan is our family genealogist, and over the years she had amassed a good number of official documents pertaining to our ancestors, including death certificates. Death certificates typically contained the names and birthplaces of the decedent's parents, revealing previously unknown names that allowed her to trace back through the generations.

A few years ago while speaking on the phone she mentioned an ancestor as I sat in front of my computer. I googled his name and city and was surprised to get a hit. I asked her for a few other names and dates, and over the next few weeks I performed searches online that provided us a fuller picture of some of these people.

Besides providing nuts-and-bolts information as to how to go about conducting your own search, I include in this volume much anecdotal material as a way of illustrating my methods and successes, as well as some dead ends, and to show how I utilized a chance or seemingly inconsequential discovery from one source to successfully search another unrelated or unexpected source and turn up something remarkable.

As an example, it was discovered in a vintage newspaper that my politician-ancestor had marched in a parade held at the opening of the 1901 Pan American Exposition in Buffalo. I had also read previously that he was an incurable jokester, and also due to a leg injury suffered in his youth, he walked with a pronounced limp. I researched the Thomas Edison films that had been shot at the Pan Am Exposition that the US Library of Congress had uploaded onto YouTube, and there he was, joking and limping along with his alderman colleagues.

Hopefully such personal information pertaining to my research, and the many things I learned along the way and continue to learn, can encourage and benefit the reader.

Searching For Your Ancestors

A great adventure awaits those setting out on the journey of a lifetime — that of discovering their origins. Unearthing, so to speak, ancestors they never knew they had, and becoming better acquainted with relatives about whom they have only hazy memories.

The goal of this book is to reveal far more than its money's worth of methods, secrets and tricks, as well as dead ends and pitfalls, to aid in researching your family history.

Building your family tree will perhaps help reactivate long-dormant instincts, namely the thrill of the hunt, as you begin to uncover completely unknown or previously only anecdotal information. Finding out that a family rumor or fable is actually historically accurate can be a thrilling experience, and knowing that it was *you* who made that discovery, also quite empowering. As we journey through this process we can also begin to discover what fine detectives we are, something that for many of us with no previous detective experience comes as a revelation.

It can't be stated strongly enough that some of the most important and satisfying finds will come as a result of first uncovering something seemingly mundane or inconsequential, such as the name of a previously unknown relative included in the newspaper death notice of a known deceased. Many will be tempted to overlook such a minor detail in their quest for The Big Reveal. But some of the greatest stories about our ancestors can sprout from just such a seemingly minor clue.

Label and file everything no matter how humdrum. Because your collection will become unwieldy you should become anal about labeling and filing.

Planting Your Family Tree:
Begin With The Living

1. Gather everything you already have — news clippings, papers, photos, documents, birth certificates, organization memberships, pins and badges, family heirlooms, awards — the list of possible clues is unique to you and your family. These materials form the foundation of your search. Many valuable clues will come from the lips of living family members as they recount their personal remembrances. Even their most mundane recollections might hold a crucial clue.

2. Question all your relatives about what they might possess of the above items. Plan a get-together so you can sort out and remind each other of what still exists from your family history. Have a scanner at the ready to make copies. In many families much has already been lost due to lack of interest of those who inherited boxes of memorabilia, which were then tossed in the garbage or donated or sold at yard sales or on eBay.

3. Rifle through your own drawers and closets, bookshelves, into long-closed boxes, the attic and basement, the filing cabinet. Check with your relatives to see if they have any family documents they are willing to share. Clues to your family history might be found handwritten on the backs of old photographs, in ledgers, day books and diaries, the family bible, news clippings, funeral cards, old postcards, membership cards, worker IDs and greeting cards. Your relative might not want their collection to leave their possession, so arrange a date when you can load up your scanner and computer and pay them a visit. Scan the backs of photos if there is any writing there at all. A name or a word that yet means nothing to you today may turn out to be crucial information down the road.

4. Interview your relatives and record the conversations. Family lore might be just that, or there may be a lot of truth to it, so don't discount tall tales entirely. Get them recorded for future reference. Begin with your oldest living relatives and then move on from there. More distant relatives such as second cousins might have knowledge your immediate relations do not. Interviews can be uncomfortable as many people have secrets they don't want to disclose, so in the beginning consider keeping questions general and non-threatening. Begin with the basics, such as, "Where and when were you/your parents/ grandparents/uncles/cousins etc. born? What was the location of their birth?" etc. Neither of my grandmothers would answer my direct questions, but I was able to gather information in an indirect way by getting them to talk about things in their past on their own terms. They would sometimes mention someone from their past who was unfamiliar to me, and I would smile and say, "Oh, she seems like she was a very nice person (or a real bitch)." That would prompt them to tell me more about that person and would often lead to other valuable clues and information.

5. Record or write whatever you learn from your family. Enter pertinent information in a family tree or pedigree chart to see how everyone connects. Pricey membership websites such as Ancestry.com allow for intricate searching, easy creation of a family tree and tidy organization of names, photos and materials -- but so do free sites such as *www.familysearch.org* . Lots of free and affordable genealogy software programs are available as well: enter terms like "free genealogy software" into search engines to find lists and customer ratings.

6. *www.familysearch.org/* is a website from the Church of the Latter Day Saints that is extremely valuable for any genealogist, and it is free of charge. Not only can you search historical records, but they have many tools and tips to start your family tree and keep it expanding.

7. Some genealogy coaches recommend beginners stick with just one surname at first, to keep from getting overwhelmed. But in reality, information will arrive when it arrives, not when it's convenient for you, so materials must be properly labeled and archived at once or risk being lost. The best way to save online finds is to create a folder on your desktop with subfolders for each surname so you can easily drop found materials into it to retrieve and organize later.

8. Alternately, you may consider rather than saving everything digitally that you also go the paper route, or at least make paper copies of the most important finds. This is recommended since digital data can be easily lost or destroyed — as computer crashes and the flaking-off of the silver coating on CDs is now proving — or become obsolete, such as floppy discs, zip discs and other older technologies. Keep copies of everything you find in your search. What may not seem important now may prove priceless in the future.

9. Regarding North American ancestors, you may find the real challenge will be in determining where and when your ancestors first arrived in North America, and from where exactly. If you're American, don't assume your ancestors directly emigrated to, or lived in, or remained in, the United States. Many immigrants moved on from the US to Canada or Australia, or moved back to the Old Country. Others arrived in Canada first, then moved on to the US, Australia or elsewhere. Searching sources over the border might lead you right to them. Many countries' borders, especially in Europe, have shifted

and changed dramatically in the last 200 years.
Determining exactly what city or town your ancestors
lived in the Old Country can be a challenge due to
compromised record sources pertaining to wars and
these ever-changing borders.

Entering search terms such as "find ancestors in
Romania" in Google or other search engine will help
start you on your way by returning results relevant
to your quest. Some genealogy websites are quite
specific, such as this Polish website locally dedicated to
Pomeranian genealogy:

http://www.ptg.gda.pl

Label and File. Label and File. Label and File.

Create a digital folder on your computer desktop and label it FAMILY TREE or GENEALOGY or something of that nature. Keep it handy right on the desktop rather than file it away so that new and unexpected finds can quickly be dropped into it, awaiting sorting. Create a subfolder in the FAMILY TREE folder for each ancestor whose name you currently know, and in the future for any new names you will discover. Let go of preconceived notions or conclusions that certain relatives are best left excluded. We cannot complete a puzzle if we throw away some of the pieces, such as an uncle known to be a criminal or a relative historically dismissed by other family members as a black sheep.

If you do not know how to grab a screenshot off your computer, learn how to do that right now, as this will allow you to quickly make a copy of a find which can then instantly be dropped into your FAMILY TREE folder before it gets lost:

http://www.take-a-screenshot.org/

On a Mac, pressing Command+Shift+4 will produce a crosshair where the arrow or little hand had been. Move this crosshair to the top left of the document you wish to copy, press and drag to the bottom right of that document and then let go. The screenshot of that document will appear on your desktop with the label "Screen shot…".

Now, change the label.

GIVE IT A RELEVANT NAME IMMEDIATELY: DON'T PROCRASTINATE. "1883SmithJohnMarriage Toronto" is an example. The more information you can squeeze into the title of a saved file the less frustrated you will be as your collection grows. In my case I always put the year first, if available, followed by the person's surname, then first name, followed by an event: "1894SmithJohnDrowned".

As soon a you save something pertaining to John Smith, immediately create a subfolder within your FAMILY TREE folder for that person: SMITHJOHN. Every time you find a new name, make a new subfolder for that NEW person in your main FAMILY TREE folder, surname first.

If for example you download or save a screen shot (also called a screen grab) of a death notice that lists many relatives' names, make a subfolder for each of these relatives and then make a copy of the death notice for each person mentioned in it, and drop the death notice into each named person's subfolder.

Downloads of materials, such as photos, documents, Census pages, news articles, official records etc. should always be immediately labeled and dropped into its rightful folder.

If you don't know how to accomplish certain things on the computer, search on Google for whatever that is ("how do I make a screen shot?" or "how do I create a folder?") or go to *www.youtube.com/* and search for a video that shows you how.

US Federal and State and foreign Census pages contain invaluable information that I find myself referring to over and over again. I keep a separate CENSUS folder on my desktop to drop Census downloads into. They should be labeled like this: "1900CensusSmithMainSt." or "1901CensusUKHuxley Blackpool".

The year should appear first, followed by the word "Census" to make locating these Census pages easy in the future via a computer search, followed by the subject's name, then perhaps other pertinent information, such as the country the Census is from, the name of the person or family, the street or town in cases where people moved over the years, etc. Be consistent in the way you title materials so that all like titles will appear together grouped in order.

Adding spaces, dashes, periods or other separators in the file title will, unless you are absolutely consistent in this, screw up the order and complicate future search efforts to locate files. It's best to have NO spaces, dashes, periods or other separators between words and to organize the words in the file or document or download or screenshot title in a consistent way.

As you accumulate Census forms you will in the future want to compare information from one to another, and this system will put them in clear order in front of your eyes when you need to refer to them.

Later on you will see the wisdom in this folder system as things begin to become unwieldy. Items within each subfolder can be allowed to become a bit chaotic until you get the time to sort them out, but at least have all of the finds that relate to John Smith placed in his SMITHJOHN folder for starters. Label even the most seemingly-inconsequential information. These minor bits are the dots that you are trying to connect. As stand-alone items they may seem minor, but may in fact contain a name or date or fact that can lead to earth-shattering findings down the line.

Always go to a search engine like Google or Bing or wikihow.com or YouTube when you want to know how to do something. As elementary as this might seem, many of us forget from time to time. Going to a search engine and typing in "how to make a screenshot" will provide many sources that show or explain how to accomplish this. Search engines are the greatest informational boon to mankind since the Guttenberg printing press 600 years ago.

I use many Adobe software programs such as InDesign and Photoshop, and I can tell you that asking a search engine how to accomplish something in an Adobe program will provide a much faster and better answer than searching on Adobe's own obtuse, unwieldy website.

Those whose main goal is to pump up their ego by establishing they are descended from a celebrated historical figure, with no particular interest in the hundreds of other relations in their tree, are destined for disappointment. We can't pick and choose who gets to be on the family tree. We cannot disown members of our family tree. There will be scoundrels. Maybe even a hero or two. But we are not our ancestors. Nor should we strive to be an apologist for ancestors for the sole reason that we believe they make us look bad. We are not them. What they did or failed to do has no bearing on us or who we are. In my case I was thrilled to find the various scoundrels in my tree. I knew I would, since neither grandmother would reveal much of anything about my ancestors, a sure sign there was a whole lot of juicy scandal waiting for me to uncover. And indeed there was.

You might even get a novel out of the experience, as I have for my Amazon-highly-rated book *The First Ward*, which had to be expanded so far to 3 volumes in order to accommodate all the craziness and drama that I've unearthed, and am still unearthing. I am fascinated that there were so many tragedies, wild stories and criminal acts, as well as astonishing suicides and murders in my family. We all have eight great-grandparents, and each one of those eight have parents, siblings and cousins, so be prepared for surprises based on the sheer numbers.

Events involving members of your small army of relatives are documented in the newspapers, magazines and public records of the day. They have been sitting there waiting for you to discover them for as long as two centuries or more. They cannot be eradicated nor should you ever want them to be. Saints or sinners, the fact is we would not be alive today had our direct ancestors not existed and survived long enough to reproduce.

One of my four great grandfathers was a detective

sergeant with the Buffalo Police Dept., and naturally
I was stoked to find lengthy stories of his exploits
in the local newspapers of his day that are online.
But in fact some of the most important finds came
not from these lengthy-detail-filled stories, but from
brief, minor sources, such as a one-line notice saying
he was transferred from one precinct to another with
no explanation as to why, for example, or that he had
served a warrant on a prominent citizen. Wondering
the reasons, I researched these questions further
in online newspapers and found a Pandora's Box
of political backstabbing, paybacks, vendettas and
retribution that greatly expanded the story of that
particular great-grandfather and the times he lived in.
Whatever you find online, even if it seems repetitive
or insignificant, give it an appropriate title and file
it away in a proper, easy to access folder. The way in
which things you may have originally been tempted to
dismiss as minor will sometimes end up connecting in
a significant manner can be quite rewarding.

A number of one-line mortgage notices in one
newspaper revealed my widowed remarried great-
great-grandmother Mary purchasing multiple
real estate properties after the Civil War. Knowing
women had few rights or opportunities at the time
I assumed her husband or grown sons were behind
these purchases, that her name had been used as a
front of some kind. Then, a close look at an illustrated
1872 map found on the New York Public Library

website, when her sons were still kids, showed their home address having two houses side by side and both registered in her name. This made me wonder if it were possible that she might have risen from destitution in 1862 to amateur real estate mogul in 1872. Finally a crazy character-assassinating news article from 1883 surfaced that was leveled directly against her. It revealed that she had indeed bought the homes solely in her own name even though she had remarried. I have yet to learn who or what was behind this salacious news article, especially as it contained easily-dispelled factual errors. This was a great example of one question being answered while the same source posed yet another. These findings added to my admiration for her and the kind of person she was.

There are certainly some well-respected professionals out there who can do your searching for you, and they may come up with some earth-shattering stuff, but nobody cares more about your genealogy than you, or knows the small inconsequential details that would spark a connection or idea. These details may sail right over the head of a researcher, so no matter what your method, professional help or DIY, you'll only get out of your quest what you are willing to personally invest into it. Both my grandfathers died before I was born. As a kid I visited my grandmothers homes very frequently, as they both lived within walking distance. I noticed that both grandmas had framed photos on display, but none were of their late husbands. *That's odd,* I thought. And that oddity was what prompted the first questions. A surefire way to know that there's a lot of secret stuff in your family history is when people clam up. Sure enough, after my poking around in public records and online newspaper archives, my knowledge of my family exploded. Our family tree on Ancestrycom which I help my sister Barbara maintain currently has well over 300 names. Originally I could have identified no more than 25 relatives.

The primary sources for genealogical information before the internet came along were birth and death certificates. In many places in the US, death certs were a requirement long before birth certs were, so death certs are more readily available, and provide a potential bonanza of information. Since death certs ask for the names and birthplaces of the mother and father of the decedent, this information has been the golden key to going back in time to become acquainted with people I owed my existence to, but had never heard of.

However, just because there are fields on the death cert to fill in this critical info doesn't mean that the person who filled it out, in most cases a relative, has indeed provided that information. In the "place of birth" field for the parents, in most instances in my case the respondent would simply write "Ireland" rather than a more exact "Belfast, Ireland." This is maddening because without this kind of detailed information a roadblock to the past in Ireland is set up. There are ways around this in some cases, as other public records, such as newspaper death notices, obituaries, Census records and the like might provide these details. The death certificate also reveals the cause of death, so seeing the word suicide or homicide can be a shocker. But other causes of death, by way of accidents or illness, the name of a hospital, the name of the doctor, the decedent's occupation and address, can all be valuable clues that lead us along the path of becoming acquainted with our ancestors.

Birth certificates, baptismal records, house of worship records and the like will all contain valuable information that can launch us in the direction of answers or dozens of unanticipated discoveries of previously unknown relatives. Even though finding a great piece of information is a real kick, keep in mind that every piece is part of the Big Puzzle, and you will use each new finding to add to the previous bit you already knew. Not only are you constructing a fuller picture of that person, but other clues found from that source, such as a street address, place of employment, etc., can open doors previously closed.

Census records are valuable to the extreme, but beware of the many, many problems with poor handwriting, lazy spelling, odd abbreviations and the like. *Errors Are Rampant.*

Many people have had problems finding their relatives on the Census because the Census taker never bothered to ask people how their name was spelled. As absurd as that sounds, let me tell you as someone who has pored over thousands of Census pages, that it is not at all the exception. An eye-opening discovery in my search efforts has been the sheer volume of mistakes and misinformation contained in all variety of "official" government records including the Census as well as in newspaper reports. Many discoveries that I have made I owe to the fact that in searching a name I would try alternate ways to spell that person's name or would search using dates other than those I had assumed were accurate. Keep this fact in mind so that you can attempt differing ways of searching. The combination of lazy Census takers who never bothered to ask how a name was spelled — and just took a wild guess at it — and the terrible writing of some of the Census takers has meant that the information is there, but buried by the Census taker's ineptitude.

When searching on *www.familysearch.com/* or *www. ancestry.com/* or other website, even if you are certain a relative was born in 1865, give yourself a wider berth, and choose instead to search the years between 1860-1870, as an example. Mistakes of all kinds in official records are rampant. Also, avoid jumping to conclusions, for example assuming a relative was married or buried in the same city s/he lived in, or that s/he never moved away for a period of time.

Public Records

A logical place to begin your genealogical research, if you have the full names of relatives, is to procure Public Records such as birth certificates, baptismal records, death certificates and other surviving records.

Much information can be found on these forms.

Death Certificates

On most death certificates there is a space for the names and birthplaces of the parents of the deceased, revealing for many researchers a previously unknown generation of ancestry. The person filling out the death certificate is most often a child or close relative of the decedent. However, sometimes these spaces are left blank, or the place of birth is listed simply as "Ireland" or "Germany", rather than "County Clare, Ireland" or "Munich, Germany."

Other kinds of listed information may include cause of death, place of birth, how long the decedent was ill, their occupation, length of time at that address, name of doctor, etc.

In most cases you must know the exact date of a death in order to procure a copy of a death certificate from the source. Searching your ancestor's name in local newspaper archives online or at the public library might turn up a death notice which will provide the date of death as well as names of family members you might not have previously known about, as well as a church, temple, cemetery or undertaker who also might have their own records on file.

On some of the death certificates that my sister procured, the name of the person filling out the form is unknown to us despite the decedent having a lot of living relatives at the time of death. We have yet to find out why a "stranger" would be providing such personal information. The death certificates were procured by us in order to answer questions, yet in the process they also posed a whole new set of questions.

If "official" sources for birth, baptismal or death certificates prove unproductive, think outside the box for other possible sources.

No official church or city records could be found documenting my g-g-grandparents marriage, but upon purchasing my g-g-grandmother's civil war widows' pension records from the US National Archives, included in this record was a notarized letter from the priest who had performed the 1850 wedding ceremony, stating he had misplaced the official documents, and giving sworn details of the place and date of the event.

The geographical location of the wedding was surprising, and that revelation sent me in a new direction revealing that my g-g-grandmother had a married brother living in that location. Searching the local newspapers online at *www.fultonhistory.com/* turned up a hundred years worth of information about this brother, his wife, children, and grandchildren. This included wild stories about the colorful antics of his only son whose name regularly appeared in the local news. In one lengthy story the son bit off the ear of the best man at his wedding. Later, as a local police officer, he had a shootout with another cop in the middle of the town's main street.

This is the kind of gold I always hope to find in my research. While others might view such revelations about relatives as troubling or embarrassing, for me the opposite is true: the more drama and craziness I find among my ancestors the happier and more rewarded I feel.

Additionally, birth or baptismal records of my g-g-grandmother's two sons were also nonexistent, but included in her widow's pension file were sworn statements by the priests who performed the boys' baptismal ceremonies, which included places and dates. It seems that with each new revelation also comes at least one new mystery in need of solving.

Sources state that her oldest son was born in the winter of 1853 in Amsterdam NY, but was baptized two days later 300 miles away in Buffalo. How was that even logistically possible at the time, or is this just another example of the kinds of mistakes regularly found in so-called "official" records?

If you know the place of worship to which your ancestor belonged, contact the church or temple directly to inquire about what records they might have. If that particular venue has closed, try to find where the original records were transferred and stored.

The above is a great example of how just one seemingly innocuous find, properly researched, can lead to many entirely new discoveries.

Prison Records.

In my research of a real bastard of a relative, the man my widowed civil war g-g-great-grandmother remarried, I assume in desperation, I found an 1869 news story about him having attacked her and stabbing her in the neck with a butcher knife. Included in her widow's pension file was an 1866 letter written by her pension agent stating that this husband was at that time incarcerated in Auburn State Prison.

STATEMENT OF COMMITMENTS

TO THE .... PRISON DURING THE MONTH OF ....18......

Agent and Warden.

Names of Convicts in alphabetical order.		Date of Sentence.	Court.	Judge.	County.	Crime.	Term.	Expiration
Harris	James	Feb. 9. 66	Superior	Master	Erie	Robbery	1 yr 2 m.	
Hibbard	William	„ 17	O & T	Mullen	Oneida	Grand Lar.	2. 4.	
Hawkins	Albert	„ 8	„	Balcom	Delaware	„	2. 6.	
Hall	Llewllyn	Apl 10	Sueme	Tyler	Oswego	„	1.	
Halliwell	Jonas	„ 14	O & T	Welles	Steuben	Rape	15.	
Halloran	Peter	„ 14	„	Balcom	Chenango	Burg 9 Lar.	1. 6.	
Henry	William	„ 16 „	„	Boardman	Schuyler	assit with intent to Ravish	2.	
Hamilton	Willoughby	May 28	„	Daniels	Chautauqua	Manslaughter	17.	
Henry	Peter	„ 25	„	„	„	Gd. Lar.	2.	
Hall	Eli H.	June 1 66	Sessions	Hubbard	Livingston	Forgery	7.	
Hitchcock	William	„ 7. 66	O & T	Mason	Cortland	Gd. Lar 2. off	3. 3. Term	
Hoyer	Samuel	„ 8. 66	Sessions	Farrington	Tioga	Gr Larg	3.	
Hayes	Geo W.	„ 5. 66	„	Lockwood	Erie	Burglary	5.	
Hardy	William	„ 11. „	„	Dusenbury	Ontario	Gd Lar.	2.	
Henderson	James	„ 15. „	„	Murray	Delaware	„	3.	
Howard	Henry	„ 23 d „	„	Hurpitt	Cayuga	„	2.	
Hall	John C.	Aug. 9. „	„	Finney	Oswego	Carrying a Slung shot	5 –	
Hale	Thomas	Sept 20	O & T	Daniels	Chau'a	Larceny	2 –	
Hogan	Dennis	„ d „	„	„	„	Bur. + Lar.	7 –	
Henderson	William	Oct 6 „	„	Boardman	Delaware	Asst & Rape	2. 6	
Haat	Taylor	„ 12 „	Supreme	Clinton	Erie	G. L.	1 –	
Hollihaw	James	„ 13 „	„	„	„	Rape	5 –	
Hanly	William	„ 13 „	O & T	Smith	Monroe	J. Petlar.	4 –	2 Note
Haines	William	Feb 23 „	Sessions	Russell	N. Y.	G L.	4 –	
Holmes	James	Sept 24. „	„	„		Bur. 3	2. 6	
Hopson	Peter	Oct 20 „	„	Coose	Chautaug.	„ 2	3 –	
Hungerford	John S.	Nov 15. „	„	Hewitt	Cayuga	G. L.	2-6	
Hines	Thomas	Dec 4 „	Superior	Verplanck	Erie	Yd prison	2. 6	
Hargrave	John	„ 19 „	Sess	McMaster	Steuben	Burg	4. 6	
Halpine	Nicholas	„ 20 „	„	Smith	Oneida	Apt to rape	1. 8	
Harrington	Ira	„ 28 „	O & T	Daniels	Erie	arson 3 d	6. 8	

Locating nothing in Google about him, I tried *books. google.com/* which found a book listing prisoners that were released in 1867 in New York State. His name was there with his early release date, the name of his prison, and earnings received upon his release (less than $7), but there was no indication of the date he was initially incarcerated, the crime for which he was incarcerated, or the length of his original sentence.

Upon my inquiries I was told the only way to get "official" state information or records on this scoundrel was if I provided his unique prisoner's number, which so far has remained elusive.

Searching on *www.fultonhistory.com/* I also found a short notice of his being incarcerated yet again in Oswego NY when he was in his sixties.

Upon researching him, search engines led me to a website devoted to black prisoners incarcerated at Auburn NY Prison around the same time as my relative, 1865, men who in many cases were connected to the Underground Railroad. Although this seemed like it had little to do with my own Caucasian relative, it made for enlightening reading, but as it turns out did indeed lead to some answers I sought. This webpage had a contact link and I took advantage by inquiring whether they had additional records that might contain information on my scoundrel-relative. Surprisingly I received a quick answer with a jpeg of a page from the prison's records showing my scoundrel's entry. It revealed the crime, date of incarceration, judge at his trial and other details that I can use to widen the scope of my research.

This website is also an example of a source of information that African Americans researching their ancestry may have never thought of. The best thing about the internet is how it leads us serendipitously to the unexpected and valuable.

Most census records list residents of prisons, workhouses, poorhouses, Industrial Schools, mental institutions and orphan asylums. If you run into a wall in your search, you might want to see if a name appears in these lists of the institutionalized.

City Directories

Your local library or historical society may have a collection of city or town directories which can prove invaluable. There are also many city directories searchable online (search on Google for websites offering these volumes with terms such as "Amsterdam NY city directory", "Sydney NSW city directory 1920" and the like.

— It was a city directory that first revealed my g-g-grandfather's civil war army regiment; this game-changing information was provided as part of his

BELL & ELY, Real Estate, 12 Eagle Street.

932   SUL   BUFFALO DIRECTORY.   SUL

Sullek, K. Rev. asst. rector St. Stanislaus Polish R. C. Church, Townsend near Peckham.

Sullivan, Andrew, laborer, 81 Van Rensselaer
" Agnes, bookkeeper, 297 Myrtle ave.
" Ann, Mrs. 127 Kentucky.
" Ann, Mrs. Vandalia cor. Tecumseh.
" Bridget, Mrs. 17 Mackinaw.
" Bridget, Mrs. 17 Perkins place.
" Catharine, Mrs. 504 Elm.
" Cornelius, 89 Jackson.
" Cornelius, engineer Electric Light Co. h. 159 Myrtle ave.
" Cornelius, laborer, 141 Kentucky.
" Cornelius, laborer, 85 Tennessee.
" Cornelius, laborer, 43 Water.
" Daniel, 347 Court.
" Daniel, bricklayer, 34 Alabama.
" Daniel, blacksmith, 711 Scott.
" Daniel, bridge tender foot Ohio st. h. 34 Alabama.
" Daniel, carpenter, over 138 Seneca.
" Daniel, carting, 111 Hampshire.
" Daniel, laborer, 444 Ohio.
" Daniel, laborer, 710 Perry.
" Daniel, laborer, 18 Tennessee.
" Daniel, laborer, 93 Tennessee.
" Daniel, machinist, 213 Clinton avenue.
" Daniel, merchant tailor, 159 Exchange.
" Daniel, molder, 148 Exchange.
" Daniel, sailor, 105 Fulton.
" Daniel, shipcarpenter, ov. 488 Front av.
" Daniel, saloon, 174 Terrace.
" Daniel, wks. Buffalo Ice Co. h. 89 Jackson
" Daniel, J. bricklayer, 34 Alabama.
" Dennis, car repairer, 711 Scott.
" Dennis, clerk 451 Washington. h. 113 Scott.
" Dennis, laborer, ov. 86 Commercial.
" Dennis, laborer, 127 Kentucky.
" Dennis, laborer, 34 St. Clair.
" Dennis, laborer, 344 Tonawanda.
" Dennis, laborer, 9 Vincennes.
" Dennis, shoemaker, 38 Swan.
" Dennis F. conductor D. L. & W. R. R. 293 Eagle.
" Dennis W. engineer, over 454 Elm.
" Edward, w. Buffalo Ice Co, h. 347 Court.
" Edward, carpenter Buffalo city water works, h. 501 Front avenue.
" Edward F. clerk W. N. Y. & P. R. R. 84 Exchange, h. 369 Thirteenth.
" Edward F. works M. H. Birge & Sons, b. 464 Front avenue.
" Elizabeth, dressmaker, 519 Virginia.
" Ellen, Mrs. over 82 Lloyd.
" Eugene (Eagan & S.) 163 Water, b. 141 Erie.
" Eugene, grocery and saloon, 210 Mackinaw.
" Eugene, laborer, 242 Katharine.
" Eugene, laborer, 11 Pioneer.
" Frank T. lumber inspector, 185 Fourteenth.

Sullivan, Frederick M. lumber inspector, 185 Fourteenth.
" George A. clerk general superintndents office W. N. Y. & P. R. R. 84 Exchange, b. 96 West Mohawk.
" Henry, laborer, 55 Columbia.
" James, architect, over 876 Broadway.
" James, car repairer, 148 Vincennes.
" James, bartender, 497 Perry.
" James, laborer, 195 Fourth.
" James, laborer, 11 pioneer.
" James, special 2d precinct, b. 16 Hamburgh.
" James Jr. lumber inspector, 148 Vincennes.
" James O (S. & Pinck) 71 Edward, h. 803 Washington.
" James V, molder 157 Church, b. 89 Jackson.
" Jeremiah, blacksmith, rear 214 Miami.
" Jeremiah, fireman, 352 Alabama.
" Jeremiah, laborer, 136 Chicago.
" Jeremiah, laborer, 142 Front ave.
" Jeremiah, laborer, 87 Kentucky.
" Jeremiah, laborer, ov. 22 Vincennes.
" Jeremiah, stonecutter, 44 Moreland.
" Jeremiah J. printer with Bigelow Pub. Co. h. 223 Swan.
" Jeremiah W. chief operator Postal Tel. Cable Co. b. Stafford House.
" Jerry, laborer, rear 742 Perry.
" Jerry, wks. City elevator, 106 Vincennes
" Johanna, Mrs. 175 Fourth.
" John, 172 Front ave.
" John, bricklayer, 34 Alabama.
" John, car repairer, 74 Fillmore ave.
" John, clerk 260 Main, h. 14 Hibbard.
" John, conductor D. L. & W. R. R. ov. 1140 Lovejoy.
" John, driver Buffalo Street R. R. b. 973 Niagara.
" John, hack driver, 78 Clinton.
" John, iron shipbuilder, 187 Kentucky.
" John, laborer, 5 Deshler.
" John, laborer, 621 Elk.
" John, laborer, ov. 332 Katharine.
" John, laborer, 773 N. Division.
" John, latiorer, 309 Otto.
" John, laborer, 7 Preuatt.
" John, laborer, 9 Vincennes.
" John, lumber inspector, b. 148 Vincennes
" John, machinist 900 Perry, h. 424 Fulton
" John, peddler, 515 Genesee.
" John, painter, rear 161 Kentucky.
" John, patrolman 10th precinct, h. 492 Front ave.
" John, scooper, 345 Fulton.
" John C. car reporter, 219 Mackinaw.
" John J. carpenter, 221 Herkimer.
" John J. furnace heater, 35 Brinkman.
" John J. letter carrier, 421 Otto.
" John, J. laborer, 22 Peacock.
" John P. (S. & Nunan) h. 12 Hamburgh.
" John S. baggageman West Shore R. R. h. 265 Front ave.
" John S. patrolman 2d precinct, b. over 508 Niagara.
" John T. machinist, 39 Maryland.
" John W. laborer, rear 429 Fulton.
" John W. machinist, 501 Front ave.
" Jonas, 220 Smith.
" Joseph, laborer, 217 Hamburgh.
" Joseph M. w. W. U. Telegraph Co. b. 50 Front ave.

directory entry.

—We traced the history of ownership and the various incarnations of a property an ancestor once owned via advertisements in city directories spanning fifty years.

—We discovered through city directories that my widowed g-grandmother for many years operated a grocery store just down the street from her house.

—In early US census records (1850, 1860, 1870) no street addresses are provided, but by cross-referencing names of an ancestor's neighbors as recorded on the US census with their entries in the city directories around the same year we could pinpoint where his family lived, as directory listings did provide street addresses or close approximations.

—The US Census revealed that a great-grandfather was a butcher by trade. The city directories from that time revealed he operated his own butcher shop and provided the street address of his shop.

—A relative who was shown in the city directories to be often living away from his wife and children, and whose occupation changed with just about every entry, gave us the impression he was a no-good. Further research revealed he was shell-shocked from his World War I service in France and suffered throughout the rest of his life from crippling PTSD. The lesson for us was not to jump to conclusions too quickly.

In documenting city directories, the microfilm maker might have been lazy or sloppy in his reproducing the directory on film, such as by cutting off part of the page — usually those names closest to the book's gutter. In one directory I found that the first few letters of the names of entire pages of entrants had been cut off, so searching by last name was impossible and showed zero results. The OCR software can only read what it can see. Knowing for certain that there were a hundred or more families in the directory having the same surname I was searching for, it was obvious to me something was amiss. I had to laboriously pore over the directory in order to find the name I was searching for, and on the correct page I saw that the first letter of their last names were all missing, as the book was not held flat enough when photographed to include the letters closest to the book's gutter. So, everyone named Smith was listed as "ith", and in fact this same problem with deleting the first letters of the last name occurred throughout the book.

Searching for old maps of the city on the New York Public Library's website I was able to find one from 1860 which showed the features of my ancestors' neighborhood, including outlines of all the structures existing in 1860, which allowed me to narrow down to three or four structures the possible houses they may have lived in. Incorporating this information, a modern view on Google Maps / Satellite View or Bing Maps /Bird's Eye provided an aerial view of what the neighborhood looks like today. Google Maps' "Street View" allowed me to "drive" right past this inexact address and explore the neighborhood as it currently exists, which as yet includes a number of very small, very modest, very old wooden houses. Did my Civil War-era ancestors live in one of these very same houses? For me it poses a tantalizing question.

Historical Societies

Buffalo has an amazing Historical Society housed in a classically-styled building preserved from the 1901 Pan American Exposition. Two relatives, I discovered after much online research, played pivotal roles in the city's history for over 50 years, yet this excellent Historical Society had practically no material on either of them.

In my case, since the Historical Society was one of my earliest stops, I thought briefly at first that I may have overestimated the relatives' importance based on the society's lack of material on them. But researching afterwards on *www.fultonhistory.com/* I quickly uncovered an avalanche of news articles — well over two thousand — spanning fifty years and containing a wealth of material about these two career politicians.

By researching further through the Historical Society's collection it was interesting to learn that in the past, the area's prominent politicians were looked down upon by society and were not included in any lists of important local citizens. This seemed to explain the disinterest of the Historical Society during my relatives' era in preserving materials related to them and other politicians. Politicians were regarded as transitory, many holding office for only a brief period, and quite a few being employed as blue collar workers in their day jobs. My own politician relatives were particularly corrupt and regarded by many in their day as little more than thugs — powerful thugs who altered the course of the city's history, but thugs nonetheless. During their era, only the cream of society were regarded as important enough to be worthy of documenting and preserving.

My lesson from this was that in retrospect there was little connection between the historical importance of a person, their role, or a particular place, and the material about them deemed worthy of being collected or that has survived. Your local historical society can be a bonanza, as even if it does not have material pertaining directly to your subject, it will certainly provide a lot of peripheral material and clues that can enrich your knowledge, provide new ideas and directions, and expand your search.

Libraries

People still love to claim that paper will, any day now, disappear. The fact is, both paper and digital have their advantages, something that will never change. It was once thought that the invention of radio would replace phonograph records, newspapers, and even live theater. In the 1950s, movie-going plummeted due to the popularity of television, and it was confidently predicted then that movies would die out.

My many hours of researching city directories online proved an arduous endeavor. Going to the library instead and grabbing a stack of directories and quickly flipping through them turned out to be far faster and more productive, and allowed speedy, rewarding side-by-side comparisons between two or more volumes that online searching did not.

On the opposite side, going through newspaper microfilms at the library might make you want to rip your hair out, as opposed to searching news pages online using OCR (optical character recognition software).

Having the paper item in your hands at the library — a book, catalog, directory, magazine — has its own distinct advantages over digital. Although you might prefer one over the other, using both and being comfortable with both will speed up and exponentially multiply your findings. In your research you cannot afford to reject either.

Many libraries maintain a scrapbook collection consisting of news clippings arranged alphabetically or by date, allowing researchers to locate news items more easily than by scrolling through microfilms. Ask at the librarian's desk if they maintain a scrapbook collection and how to best take advantage of its contents.

A troubling trend in public libraries has been book sales, whereby historical volumes of great importance to researchers, but which had not been checked out much in recent years, are sold off. This has contributed greatly in the decline of our general knowledge of history and more specifically, our research opportunities.

One local library has a section of books which the librarian himself purchased from just such sell-offs, books that he has rescued and generously makes available to researchers in his public library location. This far-sighted librarian is a great example of someone who does not mistake unpredictable periods of waning interest in certain subjects such as local history with long term value.

That other local libraries did not recognize the importance of retaining these materials is a troubling reflection on them and their stated purpose in our society.

History is an odd thing, whether it's the found history of our own ancestors or the widely accepted version of some past international event. History is indeed "his story", depending on the source.

Oftentimes a more resonant version of the history of a historical event, which may be in opposition to the popularly held version of that same event, exists in plain sight, yet little attention is paid to it. The American invasion of Canada by the Fenian Army in 1866 is one good example of this. The most widely accepted stories related to it, both the Canadian and the American versions, are politically skewed and deeply flawed.

Upon reading the stories in competing city newspapers of the same event featuring my ancestors, I have been perplexed to find two profoundly differing versions of the exact same event, at which the reporters sat side by side, yet seemingly witnessed something entirely different from each other. Even the direct quotes of the speaker, as recorded by the news reporters and reproduced in the newspapers, differed drastically — leaving the reader to wonder what was actually said. Which was the true version of that event, if indeed either one was? As you read stories in the archives of old newspapers — or new newspapers for that matter — keep in mind that just because it appears in print does not guarantee its veracity.

Page No. _57_   27

SCHEDULE 1.—Free Inhabitants in _1st Ward Buffalo City_ in the County of _Erie_ State of _New York_ enumerated by me, on the _20th_ day of _June_ 1860. _Patrick Delany_ Ass't Marshal

Post Office _Buffalo_ .

Dwelling-houses numbered in order of visitation	Families numbered in the order of visitation	The name of every person whose usual place of abode on the first day of June, 1860, was in this family.	Age	Sex	Color	Profession, Occupation, or Trade of each person, male and female, over 15 years of age.	Value of Real Estate	Value of Personal Estate	Place of Birth, Naming the State, Territory, or Country.	Married within the year	Attended School within the year	Persons over 20 y'rs who cannot read & write	Whether deaf and dumb, blind, insane, idiotic, pauper, or convict.	
1	2	3	4	5	6	7	8	9	10	11	12	13	14	
		Mary Donahoe	40	f					Ireland					1
		Margaret "	4	f					New York					2
		Mary Ann "	8	f					"					3
		James "	2	m					"					4
306	310	James Stanton	48	m		Laborer		50	Ireland					5
		Mary "	49	f					"			1	1	6
		William "	16	m		Sailor			New York					7
		James "	14	m					"		1			8
		Frances "	8	m					"		1			9
		Catharine "	5	f					"		1			10
307	311	Patrick McNamara	30	m		Laborer		80	Ireland					11
		Johanna "	30	f					"			1		12
		Anne "	11	f					"		1			13
308	312	Margaret O'Brien	40	f		Washerwoman			"					14
		Peter "	13	m					New York		1			15
		Abby "	6	f					"					16
		313	Bridget Blackwell	22	f		Dressmaker			Ireland					17
		John "	4/12	m					New York					18
309	314	John Sullivan	25	m		Laborer		60	Ireland					19
		Mary "	27	f					"					20
		James "	7	m					New York		1			21
310	315	Thomas Tillery	50	m		Carpenter		10	Canada					22
		Ann "	40	f					Ireland					23
		Hannah "	18	f					Canada		1			24
		John "	15	m					"		1			25
		Peter "	10	m					New York		1			26
		Francis "	7	m					"					27
		Daniel "	6	m					"					28
		Margaret "	4	f					"					29
		Edward "	2	m					"					30
311	316	Thomas McNamara	30	m		Laborer		68	Ireland					31
		Mary "	30	f					"					32
312	317	Margaret Shay	32	f		Washerwoman		20	Ireland					33
		Catharine "	12	f					"					34
		Mary "	6	f					Massachusetts		1			35
		Hannah "	4	m					New York		1			36
313	318	Mary Shay	42	f				90	Ireland					37
		Michael "	19	m		Laborer			"					38
		Hannah "	11	m					Canada					39
		Jeremiah "	6	m					New York					40

No. white males, _22_   No. colored males, ___   No. foreign born, _16_   No. blind, ___   No. idiotic, ___

No. white females, _16_   No. colored females, ___   No. deaf and dumb, ___   No. insane, ___   No. paupers, ___   No. convicts, ___

300

The Census

Census records are full of fascinating and useful data. The Census, depending on the year and country, provides us all kinds of information on our ancestors and their neighbors, such as gender, age, their and their parents' birth places, names of everyone living in the residence whether related or not, whether they took in boarders, how many children they have lost, people's occupations and employers, street addresses, whether they owned the house, what it was made of, its value, and much more, all of which provide information to fuel further searches. The US Census is conducted every ten years: 1850, 1860, 1870, etc. Many individual US states also conducted their own Census, usually mid-decade, such as 1855, 1865, 1875, etc. This allows us to get a sort of snapshot every five years of what might be going on with them.

The US Census is viewable for free at *www.familysearch.org/* and by paid subscription at *www.ancestry.com/* and *www.findmypast.com/* .

Serious searchers can begin by visiting the 50,000 links, arranged by country, here:
http://www.genealogylinks.net/

Following are a few links to various Census to get you started. Most websites require membership to search Census records, but since things are always in flux, first try searching using terms like "view UK census for free" and similar.

Canada:
www.bac-lac.gr.ca/eng/Census/pages/Census.aspx

UK :
www.ukCensusonline.com
http://www.1901censusonline.com/

Ireland :
www.Census.nationalarchives.ie

Australia:
http://www.records.nsw.gov.au/state-archives/indexes-online/census-records/1891-census/1891-census

New Zealand:
https://natlib.govt.nz/researchers/guides/family-history

Utilizing Census records we can learn quite a bit

about known relatives as well as discover names of previously unknown ancestors. Even knowing their neighbors can prove helpful. By following a logical path backward using the information gleaned from Census records we can trace back to fascinating discoveries.

In one case, tracing back through the Census for a female relative named Hannah, I first found her in the 1870 Census as a teen living with a couple having a different surname. Noted after her name was the term "A. Daughter", which I surmised meant adopted daughter. Going back in time to the 1860 Census I found her there as a child living with her father, mother and siblings. Then, searching in the mid-decade 1865 New York State Census, I found her living with her father, siblings, a stepmother, and additional siblings having yet a different surname.

Searching in newspaper archives using the name of this stepmother I discovered that she was the sister of the birth mother of Hannah. She herself had been a widow who had remarried Hannah's father after her own husband's and Hannah's mother's death. The stepmother's children by her first husband were brought into the new blended family. Further newspaper searching turned up death notices soon after for both the father and the stepmother, leaving the children orphaned. Searching the names of the orphaned siblings individually in later Census showed them all living with different local families who had adopted them.

Many tools are currently and easily available to us for making such family connections. Information contained in death certificates, newspaper death notices and obituaries, Census forms, city directories, military muster rolls, fraternal organization rolls, and the like will open the door to knowing our ancestors.

Using Census records to trace back neighbors and associates can have its own rewards, as we have been successful in contacting some descendants of these friends. They had photos, invitations, documents and stories to share that enriched my knowledge of my ancestors and the environment in which they lived.

Information gleaned from my great grandfather's 1900 Census record stated he was a police detective and that his brother, a politician, lived right next door to him. Doing a search under the politician's name revealed that he was a powerful and influential city alderman who served in city hall for a quarter of a century. This information led to many hundreds of news articles about the alderman and his family ultimately being found online at *www.fultonhistory.*

com/ expanding my knowledge of him enormously. Upon entering the alderman's name and city into the search field on *books.google.com/* , a number of books published by the city government turned up with his name attached to various positions and committees, voting records, etc. all which provided further avenues for research. In a short biography of him that I found in a 1914 book featuring prominent men of the day I initially discovered the alderman's and his brother's father's name, and the information that he had died in the Civil War. This added yet another generation to the family tree. In this biography it was erroneously stated that their Civil War father was buried at Arlington National Cemetery, which sent us on a frustrating wild goose chase for a while. We later found that he was actually buried in the Soldier's Home Cemetery in Washington DC.

Researching the name of my Civil War ancestor in the 1860 US Census I found someone with an identical name, and seeing that this man's wife and son had the same names and ages as my great-grandfather's family, I surmised this was the same man.

I cross referenced this name in the 1859, 1860, 1861, 1862, and later City Directories that I found online. Included solely in the 1862 Directory listing was his Union Army regiment. Using this information I located a Union Army Muster Roll online for this regiment, and found him listed there with corroborating information that he had indeed died in the war. Along with his name in the Muster Roll were a number of other neighbors and relatives already familiar to me from my research from the 1860 Census who played a part in connections that were made later.

Using this information I then procured his military record from the US Archives along with his wife's widow's pension application materials. These provided impressive amounts of information about them both as well as their children (my great-grandfather and his brother the alderman). I later found a more complete set of these records on: *www.fold3.com/*

As mentioned above, an important use of Census records is to determine who your ancestors' neighbors were. In the early US Census, those from 1850-1870, street names and house numbers were in general not noted, so after finding my Civil War ancestor, his wife and son in the 1860 Census, I was determined to locate where they had physically lived. There was no address or code included in the 1860 Census that might answer that question for me.

I gathered the names of those people listed on the

1860 US Census who appeared immediately preceding and following my ancestor's entry, his close neighbors, primarily the "HOH", or Head Of Household, and then cross-referenced those names with the city directory from that same year, as well as a few preceding and following years, to deduce what street my ancestor was living on.

These city directories exist on a number of websites and doing a google search ("Jacksonville FL City Directory") will help you find what you are looking for. In many areas, local libraries have a complete set.

In my individual experience the addresses in the 1860 city directory were often cryptic. Entries would read something like "John Sullivan, h. Louisiana St. nr. ERR", which translated meant, "John Sullivan, home: Louisiana Street near the Erie Railroad tracks."

Before I learned he had died in the war, I searched the 1870 Census looking for him after the war. But I found neither his name, his wife's nor his sons' in that same city ward. I assumed they had moved elsewhere after he returned from the war.

A week or so later I pored over the same 1870 Census again with fresh eyes and noticed one family whose HOH's wife and two oldest sons had the exact first names and ages as my ancestors, but were all listed under the family name of "Halloran." To confuse things there was also a toddler listed, which initially threw me further off. In the 1870 US Census, street addresses were not recorded.

With this new insight I then investigated the 1880 Census, searching for "Halloran". The 1880 Census recorded the Hallorans living with Sullivans at a stated street address with the older sons' surname now being correctly recorded as "Sullivan" rather than "Halloran". Comparing this 1880 information to the 1870 Census, and seeing that the neighbors were the same on both Census, it seemed I had solved the mystery of where my ancestors were living after the Civil War ended. It was apparent that my great-great grandmother had remarried someone named Halloran, which had to indicate that my great-great grandfather had died in the Civil War. It was a very important realization that opened a huge discovery portal in my search.

Shortly, after receiving from the US National Archives copies of John Sullivan's Civil War records, along with the Widow's Pension records filed by wife Mary through her Pension broker, I specifically discovered that John had died in 1862 of typhoid after having been shot at the 2nd Battle of Bull Run, and that Mary, my great-great grandmother, had been denied both her widow's and orphans' pensions. The army had lost John Sullivan's records, and thus initially concluded he was unmarried and without children, leaving his widow and children in a deadly desperate situation. It seemed to me that finding herself a penniless war widow with two small children in a city where all costs of living had doubled since the start of the war, and ultimately forced to fight an 18-month-long battle with the US government to receive her rightful due, she had placed her children in an orphanage. Then in desperation Mary remarried in order to just survive. Ultimately, in my discovery of what sort of reprehensible individual this Halloran character she married indeed was, hers truly seemed a desperate choice.

From there, official records and newspaper searches revealed that Halloran was in and out of jails, courtrooms and the State Prison system for decades. An 1869 news item revealed he had stabbed my great-great grandmother in the neck with a butcher knife, less than two years after his being released from Auburn Prison after serving 1.5 years for burglary and grand larceny.

As I went along I searched each new name I ran across in local newspapers retrieved from the archives of *www.fultonhistory.com/* . With each new hit, fresh knowledge was accumulated, expanded or distilled which allowed me to search smarter and more efficiently thereafter, thus allowing me to discover more and more.

IMPORTANT: In the US Census there are so many mistakes made by Census-takers that if at first you cannot find your ancestors where you think they should be, you will need to become more creative in your searching. Try misspelling their names in various ways. Misspellings of both first and last names are the number one problem on Census forms. Another Census absurdity is illegible handwriting. How frustrating to see so vividly that the government actually hired people with terrible handwriting to record crucial historical data for posterity.

Every conceivable mistake will be found on Census forms, such as incorrect ages, country of origin, people's relations to each other, occupations, etc., so if information on the Census does not jibe with the family stories you were told, weigh the possibility that the Census might be wrong. Or not. Sometimes the Census gets it right after all, and the family story is wrong. Keep an open mind, and think like a detective.

In the 1900 and 1910 US Federal Census, the question

is asked of women how many children they have given birth to, and how many were then surviving. Scanning any given page can be heartbreaking, as many women list half the children they birthed as having died.

My Civil war era relative John Sullivan's military records led me back to search on *books.google.com/* again, and a two-volume medical book turned up there that not only described in detail John Sullivan's battle wound, but featured a drawing of his ulna, or forearm bone, which had been shattered by a musket ball and had to be surgically removed. The information in the record named the hospital he was in, an online search of which led to photos on the *www.loc.gov/* website taken at the same time he was a patient there, including one with a man having his physical description and same injury. There is no proof this photo is of my Civil War ancestor, but the date, location, subject matter and wound all line up perfectly and this man bears a striking resemblance to photos of his known son, Alderman John P. Sullivan.

Another link led to other photos taken at the time my ancestor was at Harewood Hospital taken to document soldiers' injuries that were reproduced in a modern coffee table book, *Shooting Soldiers: Civil War Medical Photography By Reed B. Bontecou.* These photos are clear and fascinating and moving in a grotesque kind of way. I painstakingly searched through those reproduced online, but John Sullivan 49th NY was not found in this collection.

With my found information, my sister Barbara visited the local cemetery and asked the office manager about whether Civil War John's widow, our remarried g-g-grandmother Mary Halloran and her felonious second husband Peter Halloran were buried there. They were indeed. Their grave also contained both of Mary's children by Halloran, one whom we had already discovered and the other which up until then had been unknown to us. Daniel Halloran, the known ancestor, died at age 23, and his little brother Dennis died age 2. Furthermore, inscriptions carved on the 1885 tombstone stated that the stone was erected by my great-grandfather James and his brother John P. This is a great example of valuable information provided by a grave marker that allowed us to investigate all individuals involved and obtain enough information to subsequently flesh out their lives and get to know them a little better.

Researching back to the federal and state Census, we did not find little Dennis Halloran there as he did not live long enough to be included. But it did provide pertinent information on his brother Daniel Halloran which led to many more discoveries about him, including a death certificate with surprising place of birth, cause of death and place of death, all of which begged more questions and fueled more searching.

The Census can provide unexpected revelations. In the 1865 New York State Census, for example, there was a page included where the Census taker could write his own personal observations and give his opinions on certain stated questions about the area to which he'd been assigned. Sadly these opinions were not required and many Census takers neglected to make use of this page. But those who did so provided their observations and gave a vivid picture of war profiteering, political corruption, rampant prostitution, social problems, domestic cattle ownership (horses and cows were kept in urban backyards) and other surprising issues that must have most surely affected our ancestors' day-to-day lives.

The tools you utilize in your search are all intertwined, and you are never "done" with any of them, as each new discovery has the potential to send you back to the source with the newest information you have found, whether it be a Census, a city directory, a newspaper repository or other.

Inspired by Census findings that led to city directory findings, I next searched for old maps of the city. I was able to find a number of maps on the New York Public

Library's website which showed the physical features of my ancestors' neighborhood, including outlines or drawings of all the existing structures at that time. This allowed me to explore the many ancestors' street addresses that I had discovered. Incorporating this map and city directory information, a modern view on Google Maps/satellite view or Bing Maps/Bird's Eye view provided an aerial view of what the neighborhood looks like today. Google Maps' "Street View" allowed me to "drive" back and forth past these addresses and explore the neighborhoods as they exist today. Some of their homes from the late 1800s still stand.

The website at *www.familysearch.org/* has many state Census records viewable online. In some cases they are not searchable and must be tediously downloaded and researched manually, page by page. But for the patient, even this method can reveal surprises and serendipitous discoveries. A lot can happen to a family in the ten years between federal Census record taking, so the state Census combined with the national Census provides a window into what was happening to our ancestors at each five year mark.

Search Engines & Hacks

Most people are familiar with the major search engines, such as Google, Bing, Yahoo, etc. But not all search engines are created equal. No single search engine provides all available information for the same term, so utilizing multiple search engines in your search will produce better finds overall.

Search engines are your primary source always. Use well-chosen words or phrases when searching to find results that will be the most useful in your quest. Entering the words "research family genealogy foreign websites", for example, brings up a bonanza of genealogical sources outside the US for searching. So many options can be found online, in fact, as to seem overwhelming.

Creative searching is the key to mining new discoveries. Most people have learned how adding or subtracting just one word from the search phrase or search words can make a world of difference in the search results.

Begin with collecting basic data on your ancestors: birth dates, death dates, names of relatives, addresses, schools, clubs, awards, events such as auto accidents or fires, details listed in death notices such as the church or other venue the funeral was to be conducted from, etc. Then use this information in searching online newspapers, books, magazines and the like to find references, stories or articles that relate to them.

Searching newspaper archives using the name of your primary person of interest might bring up certain results, whereas searching using their home address might bring up an entirely different set of stories or articles relating to them, or reveal details about their parents, siblings, or previously unknown-to-you relatives such as cousins, who might have resided with your primary relative for a time; also servants or boarders.

The use of quotes allows us to search with more precision: entering "Mutual Rowing Club" — in quotes — into the search field will bring up different results than the same three words entered without quotes. Put quotes around people's names that you are searching to pinpoint your search more exactly. "John P. Smith" in quotes will bring up a more targeted result than John P. Smith without quotes.

Search on your preferred search engine or on *www.youtube.com* with phrases such as "search engine tricks", "search engine hacks", "clever search methods", and the like. All kinds of advice on how to obtain better results when using search engines will come up.

Google's OTHER, lesser-known Books search engine, *books.google.com/* is another animal entirely. Searching on Google Books produces entirely unique results from the identical search on *www.google.com/* . Google Books searches the million-plus books, leaflets, brochures, catalogs and other printed publications that Google has digitized and continues to digitize.

On Google Books I found a twelve-page magazine article from 1912 about my ancestor who was in the ice business, providing a photograph we had never before seen of him, as well as photos and technical drawings of the interior of his 1912 state-of-the-art artificial ice making facility.

Google Books can also be a great source for finding published materials related to still-existing or defunct organizations to which your ancestors may have belonged.

Also found on *books.google.com* when I entered my police detective ancestor's name were two books; one contained a letter of commendation from Chicago's then-police chief for my ancestor's undercover work at a Chicago Republican National Convention. The other was titled *Advocates of Murder* which told the story of his investigation into the infamous Burdick murder in 1903.

Searching on *books.google.com* with the phrase "Mutual Rowing Club" in quotes, an organization which I discovered the same police detective ancestor founded in 1881, brought up entries which in turn provided new clues for further searches that led to even more new discoveries.

Since Google Books adds to their collection daily, I revisit often to repeat previous searches to see if there is anything new that relates to my ancestors.

Besides searching using my Civil War ancestor's name, I also searched with related information gathered along the way, such as the name of the hospital he was in and the name of his doctor, each of which turned up valuable finds. It is important to be creative and open minded in how you search for information.

Discovering that a relative had attended a well-regarded academy around the turn of the 20th century, I found a circa 1900 illustrated brochure advertising that school on Google Books, and from the printed and photographic information gleaned from it, including school staff, place and campus building names — even the maker of the gym equipment — I googled all of these and ended up finding a website dedicated to this same academy (closed down 100 years ago) with previously unknown photos of my ancestor and his friends. Researching the information published on that website led to yet more discoveries about him, his friends, and his family.

Searching for the children of my relative the Alderman turned up marriage announcements in newspapers from the 1920s, providing me with his daughters' married names, and searching those revealed previously unknown cousins who had lived in the same small lake side town that my parents had moved to in the 1970s. I googled their address and that brought up a blog picturing a pamphlet announcing a family reunion with the names of all invitees. This list revealed yet more distant relatives who might have photos or information to share.

I did reach out to some of these 'new' relatives after Volume One of my novel had been published and had been well reviewed in the media, but they had no desire to have contact or share information. See my chapter titled *Poor Relations* for more on this phenomenon.

This following of the dots is what transforms a mere name on a family tree into a real live human individual whom you might wish you could have met in person. I persevered in following leads large and small, even those that seemed like they might reveal nothing of worth, but as is often the case, sometimes what initially seems like a throw-away insignificant detail can lead to major discoveries.

I had thought at one time, for example, that searching Canadian websites would prove a pointless exercise in my case, assuming as I did that my family had no Canadian cousins. Even though none of my US ancestors have turned out to be Canadian thus far, stories involving two family members were nevertheless found in Canadian newspapers online.

There are so many ways to search for information, and new information and sources are continually being uploaded. You may find that an old source that you felt you had already exhausted can provide brand-new information when you go back for another look. Most of the best online sources, for example *www.ancestry.com/* , *www.familysearch.com/* , and *www.fultonhistory.com/* , are continually adding new archives, making their usefulness ongoing.

The importance of being creative with your search terms cannot be stressed enough. However, the *greater* the number search words you type into a search field at any one time, the *fewer* relevant results will be found. Experiment with a minimum number of carefully targeted words. In addition to searching for ancestors by name, try also searching known dates, events, addresses, places of employment, etc.

You should consider your genealogical search a continuous open-ended endeavor, rather than thinking of it as a task that has a projected end-date.

The possibilities of what can be located or stumbled upon using search engines is almost infinite. The best results will be attained when we develop a personal strategy that more resembles a surgical strike rather than a scattershot approach. Search often and creatively, and then search again those sources already searched, as any change in search terms, or the adding of new material, can make all the difference.

THE ONLY NEWSPAPER IN NIAGARA FALLS HAVING A FULL LEASED WIRE TELEGRAPHIC SERVICE

NIAGARA FALLS GAZETTE

8873

VOL. XIX—NO. 273. TEN PAGES. NIAGARA FALLS, N. Y., MONDAY, FEBRUARY 5, 1912. TEN PAGES. PRICE ONE CENT.

KNEELING IN PRAYER, WOMAN AND TWO MEN GO TO DEATH WHEN ICE BRIDGE DISINTEGRATES!

Worst Catastrope in History of Scenic Niagara Marks Passing of Natural Structure Yesterday--Death for Cleveland Boy and Toronto Couple at End of Awful Hour of Anguish and Futile Efforts at Rescue by Firemen and Citizens of Both Sides of the Gorge--May Close Ice Bridge to Public.

The passing of the ice bridge yesterday afternoon, with the accompanying loss of three lives, was the worst accident in the history of Niagara as a scenic resort.

There have been numerous accidents and fatalities in and around the falls of Niagara, but at no time have three lives been the toll of the accident.

The catastrophe was entirely unexpected, and is therefore all the more astounding. Weather conditions of the past two weeks have been ideal for making ice scenery, and there wasn't the slightest doubt in the minds of anyone concerned with the parks on either side of the river and the inclined railway on the Canadian side, but that the bridge was perfectly safe.

As a direct result of the passing of the bridge, it is probable that the structure will henceforth be forbidden to tourists. Signs have already been posted on the American side, and at a special meeting held today, the Queen Victoria Park Commission will undoubtedly take action which will close the natural bridge to tourists, from the Canadian side.

District Attorney Fred M. Ackerson this morning made an informal investigation, and from the facts learned, said that the State Reservation authorities had taken all the precautions necessary to protect the lives of tourists, in the posting of signs.

That the list of fatalities was not many times as great is regarded as a miracle.

THE VICTIMS.

Burrell Hecock, 17 years old, son of Mr. and Mrs. H. L. Hecock, of East 117th Street, Cleveland, Ohio.

Eldridge Stanton, 36 years old, the Nanton Apartments, Rosedale, a suburb of Toronto, Ont., secretary-treasurer of othe Stanton-Wilson Stationary Company, 50 Yonge street, Toronto.

Mrs. Stanton, 28 years old, wife of above, and daughter of Nelson R. Butcher, of No. 247 Huron street, Toronto, Ont.

When The Ice Bridge Broke From Its Moorings

May Mean the Closing of Ice Bridge to the Public

District Attorney F. M. Ackerson Makes Informal Investigation

Gazette's Complete Extra Gives News of the Catastrope

Additional Want Ads

TOO LATE TO CLASSIFY

DIED

There's Gold In Them There Old Newspapers!

Online newspapers, books, and magazines can prove to be the greatest source of detailed information about our ancestors' everyday lives. The links below provide access to hundreds of newspapers worldwide.

Don't dismiss newspapers published out of your geographical area as being irrelevant to your search, since the early wire services fed local news to newspapers around the world. For example in the late 1880s, the tiny Hilo, *Hawaii Tribune* contained stories originating from Chicago and Buffalo as well as small towns in Nebraska and the Carolinas.

Additionally, there are holes in many newspaper archives, meaning that the collections of back issues of a major newspaper of the day may be missing a few weeks, an entire quarter, or more. At *www.fultonhistory. com/* I found that the *Buffalo Express* newspaper was missing the 1903 issues from the first quarter of the year. During this time the infamous Burdick murder took place in Buffalo that my police detective ancestor was prominently involved in investigating. The murder made headlines nationwide, so I was able to get a lot of information from newspapers all around the country. I would of course had preferred the hometown version of events, as they would be more detailed. Newspapers elsewhere may have printed an article relevant to your search that you haven't been able to find in the archives of your own local newspaper.

If your ancestors lived in New York State, or visited New York State, or had their stories picked up by a New York newspaper, then the 20 million-plus newspaper pages on *www.fultonhistory.com/* could be the greatest find ever for you. There is no charge to use this site as of this writing.

Vast amounts of genealogical information pertaining to my family was discovered on fultonhistory.com. One example is a lengthy and detail-rich news story about my great-great grandfather's Civil War grave being discovered in Washington DC by his son, Buffalo Alderman John P. Sullivan. The alderman's mother did not know this information about her own deceased husband because the army had lost his Civil War records. His sons grew up knowing little about him, and certainly nothing at all about the military service which claimed their father's life. This discovery was a huge deal for them, and upon finding this detailed article on Fulton History was for my family as well.

The Fulton History website has multiple and varied ways to search, so reading and utilizing the website's FAQ is crucial to a successful hunt there. The many different search options will give you unique results for the exact same search words, so do not give up if at first you turn up nothing significant. I have used the site extensively for 5 years, and since the owner adds new material to the archive every Sunday, I yet keep turning up news articles rich with information. Much of what I found on Fulton History dot com ended up included in my trilogy novel, *The First Ward*.

Don't ignore small public notices, such as death notices or mortgage notices, as these can provide a name, occupation, address, or event that can open the floodgates. Read between the lines as well.

One cousin who died in 1918 in the global influenza epidemic was stated to have had his funeral from the hospital, which I found very odd. Further searching revealed that quarantines disallowed embalming and public funerals for influenza victims during the Great Influenza Pandemic. This search then led to another source that revealed that the cousin had been a member

71

of the world champion *Buffalo Germans* basketball team enshrined in the National Basketball Hall of Fame in Springfield, Massachusetts.

I uncovered such items as the notices printed in small town newspapers that recorded the comings and goings of their residents and guests, such as "Mr. and Mrs. James McGrady of Amsterdam are entertaining Mr. James Sullivan from Buffalo." There were dozens of visits between these families for 40 years, as noted in the Amsterdam NY newspapers on fultonhistory.com. This gave me a decades-long timeline revealing a very close familial relationship we previously knew nothing about. That information led me to search in previously unthought-of directions, beefing up what I knew about these two families, connecting the dots.

On my mother's side I found an article in a small town NY newspaper about the mysterious death in 1899 of my great grandfather's brother while serving aboard the USS Dupont in the US Navy in Bristol, Rhode Island. The story was filled with odd inconsistencies and references, making me instantly suspicious.

I took advantage of a *www.genealogybank.com* trial membership and searched Rhode Island newspapers from that era using the scant information found in the initial New York State newspaper article. I found multiple stories in Rhode Island newspapers of what turned out to be the murder of my relative by a shipmate, another sailor who was only one day away from an honorable discharge and a sizable bonus, and other very bizarre circumstances surrounding it.

Newspaper stories are not always complete nor do they agree with one another, so any time I find information in a news story, I use it to search even further utilizing the newest information, often times greatly expanding the story. As stated often here, along with any new "answers" usually come a lot more questions, which leads to more searching.

As always, search engines are your best friend. Use them to search by name for local newspapers that may be online in out-of-the-way places. Some online newspaper archives have revealed nothing in my searches while others have been treasure troves of information. I would suggest you try the free sources first and those offering a free trial on which to cut your teeth and hone your search skills. No sense paying for a source that requires a learning curve or doesn't provide you with pertinent information.

The Library Of Congress website *www.loc.gov/* has a small collection of newspapers, all searchable, but also a great collection of downloadable photographs, maps, posters, recordings of speeches and music, and other fascinating materials.

Choose your search words/terms well. Search engine terms such as "newspaper archives online" "free vintage newspapers online" and the like will turn up dozens of sources. Here are just a few links to get you started:

http://chroniclingamerica.loc.gov/newspapers/
http://www.nyheritage.org/
http://www.fultonhistory.com
https://archive.org/
http://www.genealogybank.com/gbnk/
www.newspapers.com
https://sites.google.com/site/onlinenewspapersite/ Home
http://www.cyndislist.com/newspapers/general/
http://newspaperarchive.com
http://guides.library.upenn.edu/historicalnewspapers online
http://en.wikipedia.org/wiki/Wikipedia:List_of_ online_newspaper_archives
http://libguides.bgsu.edu/content.php?pid=473666

Australia Newspapers:
http://trove.nla.gov.au/newspaper

California Newspapers:
http://cdnc.ucr.edu/cgi-bin/cdnc

Canada Newspapers:
http://www.collectionscanada.gc.ca/newspapers/index-e.html
http://www.vpl.ca/electronic_databases/cat/C92
http://historicalnewspapers.library.ubc.ca/
http://www.ourontario.ca/demo/News.html
http://www.banq.qc.ca/collections/collection_numerique/index.html?language_id=1&categorie=6
http://libguides.bgsu.edu/content.php?pid=489945&sid=4018827

Europe Newspapers:
http://libguides.bgsu.edu/content.php?pid=478027
http://www.britishnewspaperarchive.co.uk/
http://www.nationalarchives.gov.uk/records/research-guides/newspapers.htm
http://www.irishnewsarchive.com/
http://www.irish-genealogy-toolkit.com/irish-newspaper-archives.html

eBay, and
Garage Sales

Materials offered on eBay and other auction sites can be a very rewarding source of genealogical information.

Photographs, newspapers, antique items, estate items, diaries, ledgers, books — the list of possible items pertaining to your ancestor or possibly even once owned by him/her is a vast one.

On eBay you can search for photographs of your ancestor, for example, by entering his or her name in the general Search Field.

For example, entering the name Frank Sutherland IN QUOTES ("Frank Sutherland") will take you to a page with a menu on the left of the page listing all the categories "Frank Sutherland" appears in, including perhaps Collectibles. This Collectibles section may have many subcategories, including "Photographs." Click "Photographs." and it will take you to the

Photographs section where there may, or may not, be a Frank Sutherland photograph listed.

Entering the term Frank Sutherland WITHOUT quotes on eBay will bring up a much broader selection of items containing BOTH the words *frank*, and *sutherland*, in the title, such as a photo titled "The Gang eating franks at Sutherland Lake."

If nothing comes up, eBay will tell you ("0 results for 'Frank Sutherland'"), but while you are there on that page, choose "Follow This Search" near the top of the page. Through this passive and automatic method eBay will send you an email alert whenever the term "Frank Sutherland" shows up in the item titles posted in the Photographs section.

When I first got the idea of searching on eBay (a site with millions of items) for materials related to my family, I thought it would be quite a long shot to actually find something. Since then I have made two direct finds and countless related finds.

Using eBay's "Follow This Search" feature, which notifies you by email if your chosen search term produces a hit, I found a cache of photos and documents from the estate of a cousin I never knew existed. It contained pictures of our shared great-great grandmother and other family members, as well as documents and letters. I had entered a few ancestors' names in "Follow This Search" two years previous to this find and checked out each notification consistently for two years without any relevant result. Then one day, *bingo*. This unknown cousin was a descendant of my g-g-grandfather, whose name I had entered into eBay's search notification, and thus I was notified when this estate grouping came up. The seller had — intelligently — entered the name of my relative in their item heading. This just seems like common sense of course, but many clueless eBay sellers neglect to include such vital information in their item title or even their item description.

Included in my late cousin's cache were postcards and Christmas cards from "Cousin Gregory Peck" dated 1953 when he was in Rome starring in the film Roman Holiday with Audrey Hepburn. No one in my living family had a clue that we were related to the famed actor. This association opened up a vast network of new names, since Greg Peck's side of the family had a massive family tree posted online. The crazy thing is this unknown cousin died in the late 1980s, but the estate find was listed on eBay over 20 years later. Where was it hiding all those years? And what other items might have been separated from this small collection during those 20+ years which may have provided many more clues and answers?

Another find was in relation to my paternal great grandfather, a police detective, and his lifelong friend who was also his police captain. I initiated a search notification on eBay for the police captain's name which one day turned up that captain's Police Telegraph Logbook for sale, with handwritten entries made throughout the day back in 1909 whenever a call came in to the police station for an assault, lost dog, stolen bicycle, or accident. I found an entry in it for a call from yet another ancestor, my great grandfather on my mother's side, reporting a theft which provided me with his place of employment and thus opened up a whole new avenue along which I searched and discovered amazing things about this maternal ancestor as well. In addition, the entries, made hourly as they were, gave a fascinating window into the day-to-day goings on in the city and at the precinct station itself, providing colorful details for my novel *The First Ward.*

Another eBay find was a huge bound folio of a local newspaper dating from January 1, 1909 to March 31st 1909 which had once belonged either to a public library or to the newspaper office itself. Besides making for fascinating reading, the newspapers revealed that famed world heavyweight boxer John L.

Sullivan, who via family lore we had all continually been told we were related to, was the guest of honor at a big event organized by my great-grandfather at his Mutual Rowing Club, thus bridging the connection.

Keep in mind that eBay does not allow for alternate spellings or misspellings. For example, if your last name is Halloran you probably already know there are a half a dozen alternate spellings and misspellings, i.e., Halleran, Hallaran, Holleran, Hollaran, etc. Since Halloran is an ancestor of mine, I have set up an eBay alert for every common misspelling, because I have already found that same ancestor's name spelled alternately in various government records, news articles, muster rolls, prison records and indexes.

If your ancestor's name is an unusual one, such as "Winston X. Jakeuwitz", you will have quite a search advantage over those whose ancestor is named "John Smith," since there will be an avalanche of "John Smith" materials listed that will require your plowing through, but relatively few for "Winston X. Jakeuwitz."

The more common the name or term, the more clever you must be in finding ways to narrow your search to find the correct relative. Most eBay auctions are 7-day auctions, so to save time, normally I will only check out each of my alerts once a week, since checking each daily would require quite a bit of time.

A huge issue to be aware of on eBay is clueless sellers who do not include an ID in their headline even when an ID clearly exists. When a photo has "Mary C. Johnson, 1904, Michigan Ave., Chicago" handwritten on the back of it, and the seller lists it with the title "old photo of angry looking girl" — which happens so often on eBay as to be exasperating, by the way — it makes me want to request eBay ban them forever for being Too Stupid To List. It doesn't occur to these mindless sellers that buyers are searching for specific names, dates and places, not generic photographs of "angry looking girls."

Ebay has some intelligent features, but recognizing misspellings in the helpful way that Google or *www. dictionary.com/* recognizes them is not one of them. Currently, if you search eBay separately with the terms "Niagara" and "Niagra", each spelling turns up an entirely unique set of items for that same geographic place. When looking for something specific, try being creative in your search by searching with a misspelled or foreign version of the word. Searching on eBay with the word "Hawaii" brings up one group of items, but searching with the European spelling, "Hawai" brings up a entirely unique group of Hawaii items, since in many foreign languages it is spelled with only one "i".

"Colour photo", the British spelling, brings up different results than "color photo". However "NY photo" not only returns photos listed as "NY photo" but also returns many "New York photo" listings as well.

Unless your preferred eBay search term is included in the title that is supplied by the seller of the item, the item won't turn up, even though it might be listed. If you have a preferred eBay search for "political button," for example, items that are titled by sellers as "political pinbacks" or "political badges" — all interchangeable terms for the exact same thing — will not come up. "Det. Smith" will not find items labeled "Detective Smith." "Aldermen" finds items different than "Aldeman." "Mr." will bring up different items than "Mister."

When searching on eBay for a specific item, think of what other names or terms this same item might be known by, and add that to your "Follow This Search" list. Ebay is international, and foreign words for the object are worth looking up. In the UK different English words are used for familiar objects known in the US: automobile trunk = boot; sweater = jumper, etc. A helpful source for determining some alternate names for the same object is *www.thesaurus.com/* .

As another example, when I search on eBay using the word "rowing" in quotes, sellers' titles containing that exact word come up. But if I search on eBay with the word *rowing* WITHOUT the quote marks, it will bring up a spate of items that are totally unrelated to rowing, such as concert tickets titled "Rolling Stones Row 26, Seat 14." Using quotes helps to keep the search from wandering too wildly off the intended path.

One thing I must emphasize repeatedly throughout this book is the importance of the Inconsequential Detail. Some seemingly minor bit of information can open up an entirely new discovery for you, such as in my case the notation of my ancestor's call in the 1909 police captain's log. Your skill as a detective will be tested by recognizing when this occurs, rather than overlooking the clue.

In your online searches regarding your ancestor on eBay, in newspapers, public records, obituaries, etc. using misspellings of the name can oftentimes result in an exciting breakthrough, since misspellings. OCR glitches, and typos are so common. When searching newspapers on *www.fultonhistory.com/* , one of this website's options is to allow for misspellings, and invites you to set the strength of the filter in "fuzzy search."

Local garage sales, estate sales, antique markets and swap meets have the potential to turn up all kinds of materials and possessions that would be of great value to your genealogy collection. Neighbors' estate and garage sales especially have the potential for discovering photographs and other materials.

My sister Barbara stopped at an annual antiques sale near her home and encountered a seller who specializes in localized New York State books and ephemera. He had it neatly orgnized in boxes as to location and in a box of Buffalo materials she found a beautiful multi-page fancy menu for a banquet held in 1915 upon the retirement of our alderman ancestor.

She also attended an estate sale of a former neighbor and scored the neighbor's photo album that had photographs of us and our siblings as children that we had never before seen.

Barbara volunteers at a very small localized museum devoted to just one area of the city. There she meets people coming in to do research who provide her with stories, photographs and connections that pertain to our own family and provides others with knowledge that help them in their genealogical research. Ask around or do an internet search for just such localized resources in your area.

YouTube.com

YouTube's website www.youtube.com/ has a vast repository of viewable films, videos, slide shows and sound recordings, and is a rich resource often overlooked by those researching their genealogy.

The US Library of Congress has uploaded its collection of early motion pictures to youtube, most of these produced by Thomas Edison. Edison's films of the 1901 Pan American Exposition in Buffalo caught my attention after reading in a vintage newspaper that my ancestor, who was a prominent city alderman, marched in the opening ceremonies behind Teddy Roosevelt. Reviewing the films on youtube with the knowledge that a leg injury in his youth left him with a severe limp, I was able to view him as he joked with his fellow alderman walking in the parade.

Another Edison film's subject was the annual Police Parade in Buffalo in which seemingly every second participant bore a strong physical resemblance to my police detective great-grandfather, and thus I have not been able to identify him individually. However I cherish the film anyway as I know he's in there somewhere, and seeing his fellow police officers in their turn-of-the-century environment is ultimately satisfying.

The British Film Institute also has uploaded a vast collection of early films on youtube. Most interesting are their early color movies from the 1920s filmed from moving vehicles as they plied the streets of London and other towns. Most people are unaware that color movies go back to the late 1800s, and seeing people and places from so long ago in color is fascinating. Searching on youtube will bring up many very early color films of celebrities like Josephine Baker in performance and beautiful experimental Eastman Kodak films of pretty models, bringing to life images from an era that most of us are only familiar with in black and white.

My curiosity piqued after reading in another vintage news story that an ancestor liked to sing a popular turn-of-the-20th-century song titled with our family surname, I found an Edison recording of it on youtube; "Sullivan" by Billy Murray, written by George M. Cohan.

Search on youtube and elsewhere with more than just an ancestor's name; try his/her company, school, town, occupation, hobby, street, event, award, crime, athletic ability, accomplishment or other pertinent information.

As mentioned in its own chapter, the BBC television program, *Who Do You Think You Are?* is not only endlessly fascinating, but can provide the viewer with previously unthought-of options and ideas in conducting your own family search. Dozens of WDYTYA episodes have been uploaded to youtube. WDYTYA takes celebrities in hand and leads them through their family history as has been discovered by the producers, with the celebrities visiting the towns, villages, churches, prisons and haunts of their ancestors to see, hear, feel and discover.

One disappointing thing about YouTube is how often uploaded films and sound recordings disappear and are no longer available. Free and inexpensive software is available for downloading a youtube film to your computer, in the event you find something relevant you want to preserve to show others or include in your genealogy archive. Use search engines to locate this software, entering terms such as "download youtube video software."

The US Library Of Congress

The Library of Congress website, www.loc.gov/ is an amazing repository of information available to all, free of charge. Its vast collection includes photographs, newspapers, films, maps, veterans' histories and more.

No newspaper collection can be called "complete", and the LOC's own collection pales in comparison to that of *www.fultonhistory.com/* which provides access to many scores of New York State and other region's newspapers and other research materials. We wonder why the LOC does not partner with other organizations, libraries and entities to provide a wider scope of research materials. Regardless, the LOC's limited newspaper collection *does* add to the rich mix available online today.

The LOC map collection is remarkable, especially the turn of the century "bird's eye view" maps popular at the time which picture actual buildings, including my ancestors' houses and places of business. These bird's eye maps give a vivid view of what the surroundings were like and in and of themselves provide clues and insight.

In the LOC's Photographs and Prints section, searching is easy and fast. Not everything in the collection is viewable online, such as certain photo collections, but much is. Often a number of download options are provided for any given available photo, anywhere from a small low resolution version suitable for a website or personal notes, up to super-high resolution showing enormous detail.

In my novel trilogy *The First Ward*, which is based heavily on actual people and events, I had included an interesting story found in a vintage newspaper page adjacent the story I was originally researching. It told of a black man named Michael Jackson who was a painter/whitewasher. He had occupied a spot next to St. Paul's Cathedral in downtown Buffalo for over 30 years in which he stationed his pull cart and drummed up business. His father before him had occupied the same spot for decades as well. With the coming of a huge public event, Buffalo's 1907 Old Home Week, Jackson was summarily kicked off his spot permanently by the police. The local newspapers took up the story, which had a happy ending.

In the LOC photo files I found a very high resolution photo from this time of the church where he stationed himself and downloaded it. Upon zooming in, lo and behold, there was Michael Jackson, next to the cathedral, sitting on his whitewash cart filled with his pails and brushes. I had found a photo of the actual person in his environment with which I could use to illustrate my story about him.

The LOC Photographs collection includes photographs of both everyday people from long ago as well as more modern times, including immigrants and laborers, identified by name or street address, so try searching for ancestors, events, their streets, schools or places of employment there. It might seem like a long shot, but you never know what might turn up.

fold3.com

Whether US National Archives workers are inept or just plain lazy had not yet been fully determined, but recently I took *www.fold3.com* , the military records website, up on their offer of a one week free trial and searched my civil war great-great-grandfather's records on their website. I had already paid a pretty penny ($175) for his records from the National Archives, but since I had a free trial at fold3.com, what could it hurt to look?

Fold3.com revealed almost *twice* as much information on him for free as had the National Archives provided me for $175.

The National Archives charged me $175 for a haphazard and incomplete record, while fold3 charged me nothing for a far more complete record.

The lesson learned is that not only can official records have missing parts and other deficits, mistakes or erroneous information, but the people who you trust to do their job can prove to be sloppy, incompetent, or just downright lazy.

The National Archives also told me they had no information at all on my maternal grandfather who had fought in WWI, but fold3.com did provide some information on him.

Your belief that a government archive rather than a private entity will provide you a superior result, or that paying dearly for something gets you more and better information is not necessarily correct — as my own experience has shown.

Obtaining US military records can be a problem because of destructive fires. It is claimed that virtually all World War One US military records were destroyed in a blaze, and quite a bit from WWII too. The bulk of the 1890 US Census was also destroyed in a fire, with just a small percentage surviving.

All these fires were the result of smoking. Ironic that so many of our relatives and ancestors died from smoking, and so too did much of their military legacy.

Birth, Death and Tombstones

Armed with a list of names and dates, try visiting
local cemeteries to find ancestors. Most stones provide
year of birth and death. Many cemeteries have a
records office with someone knowledgeable about that
cemetery to talk to. These employees can direct you
to graves and provide you with information from the
cemetery's written records which will contain their
own clues, allowing you to expand your ancestral
exploration.

In my case, a plot map provided by the cemetery
for my great-grandfather and his family's burial plot
revealed four unknown children there. It turned out
they were my grandfather's siblings, buried with my
great-grandparents but having no grave markers.
Three of those children died within a five year time
period. We had no previous knowledge whatsoever
of their existence or burial until we saw this plot map.
With the dated information in the cemetery's records
we were able to then find their death notices in local

newspapers via *www.fultonhistory.com* and then to obtain their death certificates to learn about how they died and other clues, such as doctor's names. A found news article revealed that one of the children had fallen off a raft into the river just yards from the family home as he played with friends and drowned. Knowing such details and other events transpiring around the same time allowed us to form a very sympathetic picture of what the family must have been going through dealing with deaths of children, workplace drama, nefarious political maneuvering that directly affected the family, troubling economic and social conditions, etc. all concurrently.

Predictably, with answers came more questions. Records from the same cemetery revealed the as-yet unsolved mystery that three deceased children of my alderman relative were not buried in his family's large plot nor in his mother's second family's plot close by, which he and his brother had purchased before they themselves had children.

In addition the cemeteries and graveyards you already know about, expand your search for buried ancestors on the very valuable cemetery resource *www.findagrave.com* which lists millions of names and hundreds of thousands of photos of grave markers. Uploading a photo of your ancestors' tombstones adds to the database and is one more way to immortalize a relative's life. Find-A-Grave allows photos of the deceased to be uploaded as well, for no charge. For a very small fee you can sponsor a large webpage dedicated to a decedent and fill it with photos, memorials and other information.

The interesting thing about graveyard headstones is that it is not unusual for the information on them such as dates and the spelling of names to conflict with other records. These conflicts might result in more questions, or perhaps may solve a previous mystery. But the question remains: why do two "official" sources so often differ in the first place?

Sometimes tombstones provide other information too. On the stone marking the graves of my g-g-grandmother and her second family it is inscribed, dated 1885, that the marker was commissioned by her two sons, an attribution not seen on any other marker there. The maker of the tombstone still to this day operates a facility right across the street from the cemetery, and recently it occurred to me that they might have kept their own records which might provide information on this or later transactions.

My sister's research showed that the young adult sister of another great-grandfather died while in the employ of the railroad and was buried in the railroad's own cemetery, despite the family owning a large plot in the church cemetery nearby. Afterward her body was disinterred and reburied in the family plot. The small town has a library but my sister's research could not provide any information on her death nor the odd circumstances surrounding her burial.

Her brother, who while in the US Navy was murdered by a shipmate in 1899 in Bristol Rhode Island, was at first buried in a cemetery in Newport, despite having a wife in Pennsylvania and living parents and siblings in New York. His body was later disinterred and moved. Continuing research has not revealed why this first burial, at the behest of the US Navy, occurred or why he wasn't immediately returned to his family.

Visiting graves and making your presence known at the cemetery can have another positive outcome. In J.K. Rowling's episode of BBC's *Who Do You Think You Are?*, she had tracked down her hero-ancestor's grave in France and traveled to the cemetery to pay her respects. Upon arrival she found that his grave was gone. It was explained that because no family had visited or made their presence known for decades, the crowded cemetery had a policy of digging up old graves and consolidating those deceased into a common grave, to make room for newcomers. They'd disposed of the decedent's gravestone as well.

PHOTO BY R. E. SHEEDY. GAWLER, S. AUS.

Who Do You Think You Are?

Besides being fascinating, the TV series *Who Do You Think You Are?* can light a fire in the imaginations of viewers, inspiring them to begin or renew their own genealogical search efforts.

The program chooses a celebrity and traces back through their family tree, finding previously unknown or little-known ancestors having amazing stories that run the gamut from chicanery, tragedy, and utter despair to heroism and triumph.

The program, by following the search process through libraries, news archives, government repositories and the like, presents a virtual genealogical how-to for viewers. The program also reveals sources that many people might not realize exist.

Having known a number of African Americans who felt that researching their ancestors would most likely prove pointless due to the lack of records going back to slavery, I learned differently watching WDYTYA. A number of black celebrities in different countries are featured and their individual, unique journeys reveal some very valuable avenues and methods by which black people, and African Americans in particular, can research their genealogy.

The most dramatic surprise for a number of WDYTYA's black celebrities is the prominent presence of white ancestors in their lineage, a mind-bending revelation they had never considered.

Many episodes of *Who Do You Think You Are?* are available for viewing on *www.youtube.com/* . There are American, Canadian, and Australian versions of the original BBC program, and some of the wildest and most emotionally touching stories are those of foreign celebrities you may not be at all familiar with, so don't prejudge or overlook a particular episode simply because you are unfamiliar with the celebrity-subject.

Interestingly, two of the British episodes featured UK celebrities who had an American connection via their ancestors' emigrating to the US, but who or whose descendants afterward subsequently returned to Britain.

In the United States, PBS TV aired a similar program titled *Faces Of America* which is available on DVD with some episodes viewable on *www.youtube.com/* .

Essential Links

Following is a list of resources that have proven very productive in my own experience. Thousands of other resources exist which I have yet to take advantage of, and thus I cannot comment on them. But those listed here have consistently provided much of great value in my research:

The Church of Jesus Christ of the Latter Day Saints:

This premier no charge / no strings genealogy website is offered by the Church of Jesus Christ of the Latter Day Saints to all comers. It is phenomenal, and non-denominational. Don't worry, no one will call you, spam you, or try to convert you, so it should be your very first stop. Their records are universal and do not favor Mormons or any other group. It is truly a free website in that visitors are not required to register or sign in to make use of its tools.

Family Search-dot-org has many US State Census free for the viewing. In addition to the federal US Census conducted every 10 years on the naught, most US states conducted their own census halfway though each decade, allowing us a fuller picture of our ancestors and what they may have been up to: *www.familysearch.org/*

USGenWeb Project:

USGenWeb Project is a group of volunteers working together to provide free access to genealogy websites for genealogical research in every county in every state of the United States. Their admirable philosophy of free genealogical resources for all comers is the backbone of their mission statement: *www.usgenweb.com*

Genealogy Links website:

Fifty thousand worldwide links abound on the Genealogy Links website. No matter where on earth your ancestors originated, you will definitely find a number of sources here to aid you in your research: *www.genealogylinks.net/*

The US Library of Congress:

The LOC website provides a treasure trove of vintage newspapers, maps, photographs, films, sound recordings and much more that are viewable and downloadable free of charge. The LOC has posted much of its century-old moving picture collection on YouTube.

www.loc.gov

Fulton Postcards:

You do not have to have New York State origins to benefit from the 20 million+ newspaper pages archived on Fulton Postcards' free website. The love child of just one single individual, Tom Tryniski, this site excels in its collection of small town, mostly New York State, newspapers from the 19th century, but its scope is all-encompassing. Vintage local NYS newspapers were filled with stories and notices from all over the world, so don't overlook this website's numerous and excellent search formulas and capabilities no matter where in the world you live. People living outside the USA should not automatically assume their ancestors were not American, or did not emigrate to the US for some period of time, or spend significant time in the United States while yet retaining their native citizenship:

www.fultonhistory.com

New York Times:

The search box at the top of the New York Times website's splash page will locate stories, names and events dating from the paper's beginnings. Since the Times' coverage has always been international in scope, don't overlook it as a source. At the time of this writing there is no charge to retrieve past NYT news stories:

www.nytimes.com

Find-A-Grave:

At *www.findagrave.com/* you can search and locate, for free, the burial places of those in whom you are interested. Volunteers have photographed tombstones and grave sites internationally and posted images on this site. My research ultimately found that my Civil War ancestor had been buried at the Soldiers' Home Cemetery on Harewood Road in Washington DC. Turning to Find-A-Grave, I found his gravestone pictured there. But the photo of his stone showed a modern granite marker as opposed to the rest of the cemetery's vintage white tablet markers. So here was another mystery that was for a while vexing, until a news story found on *www.fultonhistory.com* revealed that my ancestor the alderman, upon finally discovering his long-lost father's grave's location, had the original tablet replaced. There was no reason given as to why this was done.

You can upload images and biographies of your ancestors at no charge, or sponsor a page for them for a very small fee. Find-A-Grave is an invaluable source of research information. It also provides a way for us to immortalize our relatives or ancestors so that they will not be forgotten.

As an aside, don't overlook the helpful staff at local cemeteries in your community. Cemetery records can provide fascinating information, such as ancestors buried in unmarked graves.

Ancestry dot com:

Ancestry is a subscription service with a vast collection of records available worldwide. It is expensive, but invaluable, so the best tactic is to take advantage of their free introductory offers and periodic special pricing offers. Collect together as much data beforehand, such as names, dates, and birthplaces to make best use of your time.

Ancestry-dot-com builds a family tree and shows exactly how you are related to your ancestors (eg: "wife of second cousin twice removed"). It also offers an affordable DNA test which purports to reveal your roots by breaking down your genetic origins into percentages. Searching takes time and patience and there will be times when you hit a wall and feel you can't go any further. That might be the a good time to try other sources which can reveal information that can be used in some future ancestry-dot-com search.

Narrowly Targeted Websites:

Among the tens of thousands of websites of interest to genealogists like you and I are many projects conducted by individuals and groups that are very specific and with a very narrow focus of interest. Locating these can save you enormous amounts of research time if its area of interest jibes with your own. As an example, this volunteer-run website requires no sign-in or registration and is devoted solely to the 1901 Canada Census, providing an index to every name enumerated in the 1901 Census of Canada:
www.automatedgenealogy.com/census/

Poor Relations

Soon after my novel *The First Ward* was published and had attracted quite a bit of favorable media attention, I optimistically anticipated that distant relatives might begin coming out of the woodwork and share materials they had, such as photos, memorabilia and family stories. My novel is based heavily on fact and actual events as discovered in more than 2000 newspaper and magazine articles, photos, maps, official records and documents that I have collected over the years.

This did not happen. I wrote letters to more than twenty previously unknown cousins whose names I discovered along the way, only one of whom responded enthusiastically, and another offering an unkept promise to "talk more about this at a later date." The fact is most people have little sustained interest in their family history. Obviously they have more important things to attend to.

One previously unknown relative telephoned out
of the blue who, even though already having gleaned
a vast amount of previously unknown-to-her family
history from my book, was anxious for more. She
had a barrage of questions right out of the gate. I
hit pause and reminded her that I was interested in
getting just as much as I was giving. She continued to
evade. She related a tedious story about, then asking
me to contact, another relative with whom she was
not on speaking terms and who I did not know, to
have returned to her a set of dishes she believed were
rightfully hers. I cut the conversation short and told
her when she was ready to share equitably to give
me a call back. That was well over three years ago. I
assume she's not ready yet.

She did however contact her brother across the
country and informed him that my family had an
ancestry.com page. He immediately got online, and
without messaging us to say hello, 'sup, or thank
you, appropriated scores of photos, documents, news
articles and whatnot. I sent him a friendly message
through ancestry.com asking him to please share
what his family might have in their collection since
we'd already provided him with so much. He did not
respond, yet continued visiting our pages to abscond
with additional materials. We finally had to make
our ancestry page private since he and other distant

relatives demonstrated not just their disinterest in sharing with us, but their sense of entitlement by simply walking away with what we had so laboriously collected.

So, if you plan on reaching out to new-found relations, be ready for some crazy, or be ready for relatives who want nothing to do with you. Be ready for relatives who have little interest in providing you with any information but will be ravenous for whatever information you can give them. If you don't come from money, relatives who do have the bucks will run away screaming, convinced you've come for theirs. Some relatives will be fearful that you have uncovered their family's darkest secrets, especially if you happen to be a writer :-)

Only one relative, a granddaughter of the alderman, was enthused about connecting with us. She told me over the phone many things, but mostly that she loved my book and that she had albums filled with photos and news articles about the alderman she'd like to share. I asked her if my sister could come visit her, since I lived far away. She said she would love to meet Barbara. They set a date for less than five days after that initial phone conversation, and the day before my sister's visit, our new-found relative died.

I sincerely hope that you have better luck and an overall more cooperative set of relatives than we do, and that you can successfully engage with your own relatives to each contribute to a joint pool of family lore, diaries, certificates, sound recordings, movies, photographs and whatever else the previous generation may have left behind so that your generation and future generations won't forget who their ancestors were.

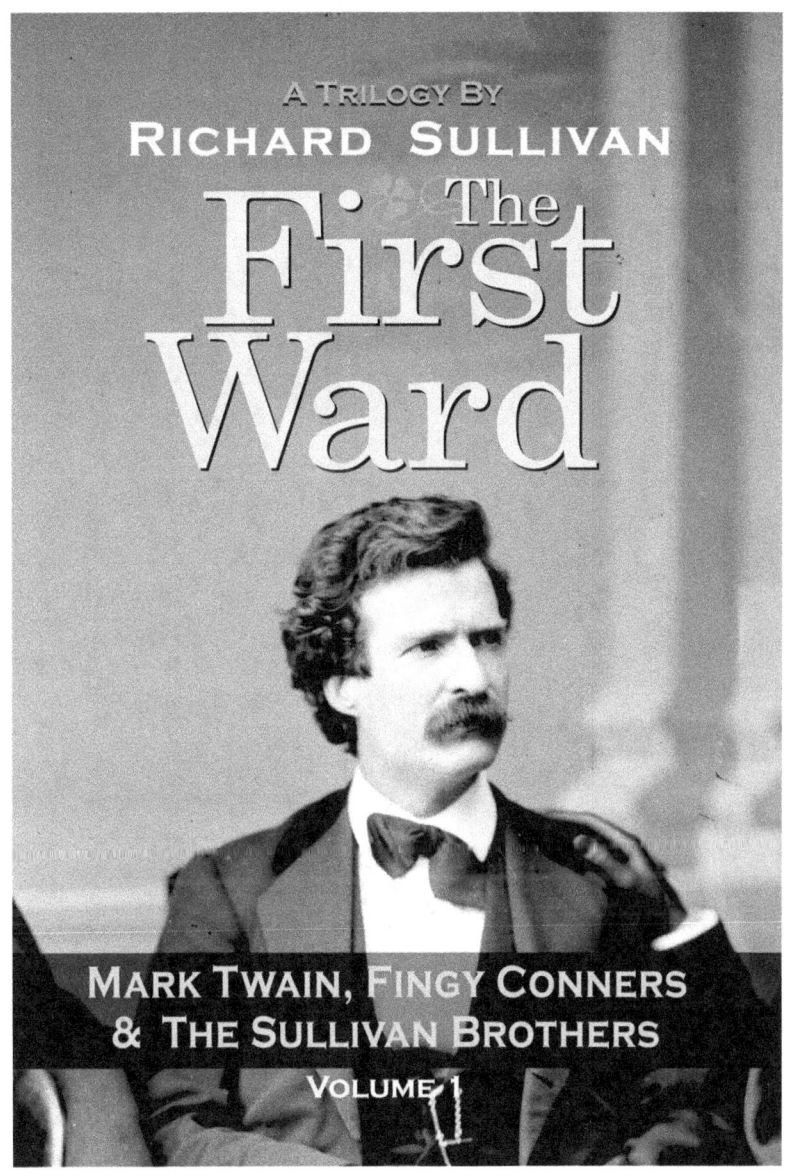

The infamous Fingy Conners begins his stunning ascent politically, all the while descending further and further into tyranny and murder.
The First Ward
is available at Amazon.com and select booksellers.

A TRILOGY BY
RICHARD SULLIVAN

The **First Ward II**

**FINGY CONNERS
& THE
NEW CENTURY**

The Saga continues in
The First Ward II: Fingy Conners & The New Century
Fingy Conners achieves unparalleled financial success and political power
through street thuggery to the detriment of all those around him.

More books by Richard Sullivan

Driving & Discovering Hawaii: Oahu
Winner, Travel Journalism Award For "Best Hawaii Guidebook" by American Airlines and the Hawaii Visitors and Conventions Bureau. Named "Best Hawaii Guidebook" by the Los Angeles Times, the Chicago Sun-Times, the San Diego Union-Tribune, the Orange County Register, the San Jose Mercury, and The Oregonian. Read the RAVE REVIEWS on AMAZON.com

Driving & Discovering Maui and Molokai Another beautiful guidebook from award-winning author and photographer Richard Sullivan. Each photo is numbered and its exact location pinpointed on an adjacent map, making this Maui and Molokai guidebook your best bet for unforgettable sightseeing and great restaurants, as well as for vacation photography and video.
"A picture is worth a thousand words... which is why the 300+ beautiful photos in Driving & Discovering Maui and Molokai guidebook make this the best available, and a real bonanza for photographers searching for their best island shots. Nobody puts the "guide" in guidebook like Richard Sullivan" -*photonet.com*

These Hawaii books are available from most Hawaii booksellers, Hawaii Airport stores, Hawaii Costco, ABC Stores and online at www.DiscoveringHawaii.com

Reclaim Your Youth: Growing Younger After 40
Science reminds us that the more robust our muscle mass, the faster we burn fat and the stronger and more agile we are. The elderly don't fall down because they're old. They fall because their leg muscles have atrophied to such a degree they can no longer hold them upright. Increased muscle mass is your guarantee that you'll still be walking—and running—when your contemporaries may be using walkers.
Looking great below the neck is just as important as from the neck up. Reclaim Your Youth isn't about magic pills or the Secrets of the Hollywood Stars, because these things don't exist.
It's all about eating less and moving more.

Search Amazon.com for books by Richard Sullivan.
Visit www.DiscoveringHawaii.com for free Hawaii maps, videos & Information.

www.ingramcontent.com/pod-product-compliance
Lightning Source LLC
Chambersburg PA
CBHW070154290526
45789CB00002B/770